Amelia Earhart
Aviation Pioneer

by Grace Hansen

Abdo
HISTORY MAKER BIOGRAPHIES
Kids

abdopublishing.com

Published by Abdo Kids, a division of ABDO, PO Box 398166, Minneapolis, Minnesota 55439.

Printed in the United States of America, North Mankato, Minnesota.

102015

012016

THIS BOOK CONTAINS RECYCLED MATERIALS

Photo Credits: Ames Historical Society, AP Images, Corbis, Getty Images, iStock, Shutterstock, © User:Hellerick / CC-SA-3.0 p.19

Production Contributors: Teddy Borth, Jennie Forsberg, Grace Hansen

Design Contributors: Laura Mitchell, Dorothy Toth

Library of Congress Control Number: 2015941764

Cataloging-in-Publication Data

Hansen, Grace.

 Amelia Earhart: aviation pioneer / Grace Hansen.

  p. cm. -- (History maker biographies)

Includes index.

ISBN 978-1-68080-121-7

1. Earhart, Amelia, 1897-1937--Juvenile literature. 2. Women air pilots--United States--Biography--Juvenile literature.   1. Title.

629.13/092--dc23

[B]

2015941764

Table of Contents

Early Life

Amelia Mary Earhart was born on July 24, 1897. She was born in Atchison, Kansas.

Kansas

Frank Hawks was a famous aviator. In 1920, he took Amelia on her first plane ride. She loved it!

7

Up, Up, and Away!

Amelia's interest in flying grew. She took flying lessons. She even bought a plane. She named it *The Canary*. It was bright yellow.

9

In 1928, Amelia was invited on a flight. The flight crossed the Atlantic Ocean. She was the first woman to do this.

The flight made Amelia famous.
But she was only a passenger.
She wanted to make the trip on
her own. So, on May 20, 1932,
she did!

Next, Amelia flew across the Pacific Ocean. Now she was ready for a greater challenge. She wanted to fly around the world! The flight would start in California.

15

Amelia and **navigator** Fred Noonan took off from Miami, Florida, on June 1, 1937. Amelia completed about 22,000 miles (35,400 km) of her trip. She had about 7,000 miles (11,300 km) to go.

Missing

On July 2, The US Coast Guard waited near a small island in the Pacific. Amelia was supposed to refuel there. She never made it. Amelia and her plane have never been found.

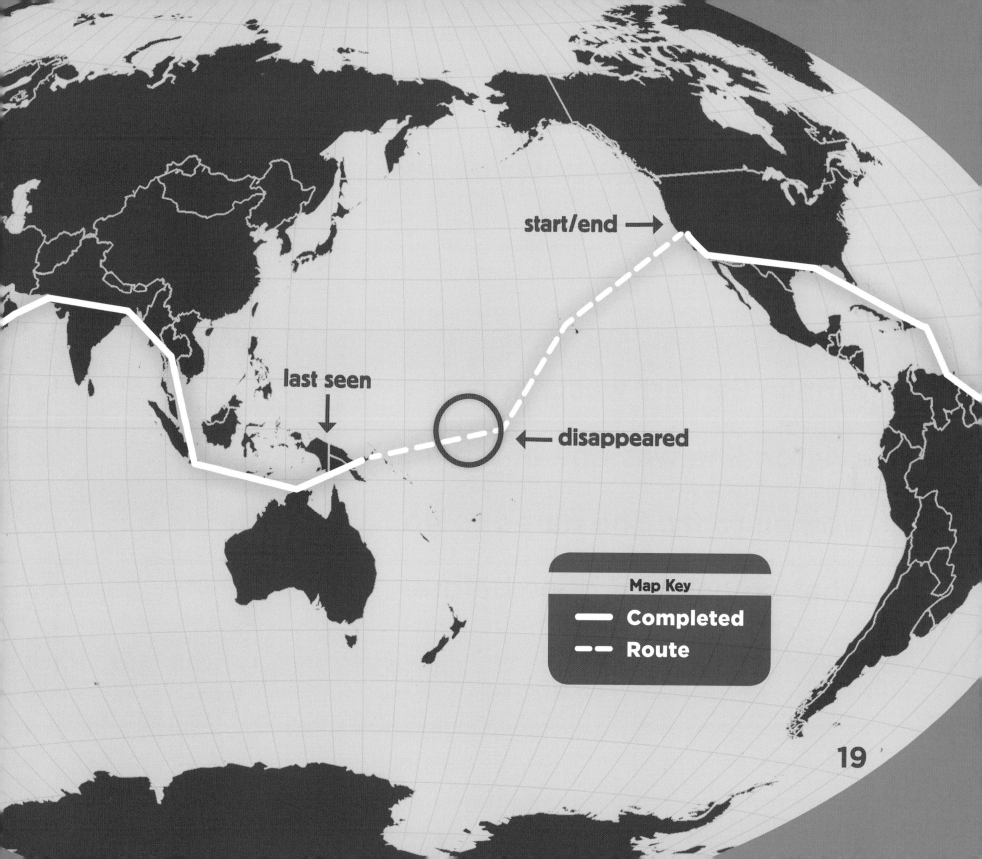

start/end →

last seen

disappeared

Map Key
—— Completed
-- -- Route

19

Legacy

Amelia Earhart was a great aviator. She was one of the first women to fly. She dared to do what no one had done before.

Timeline

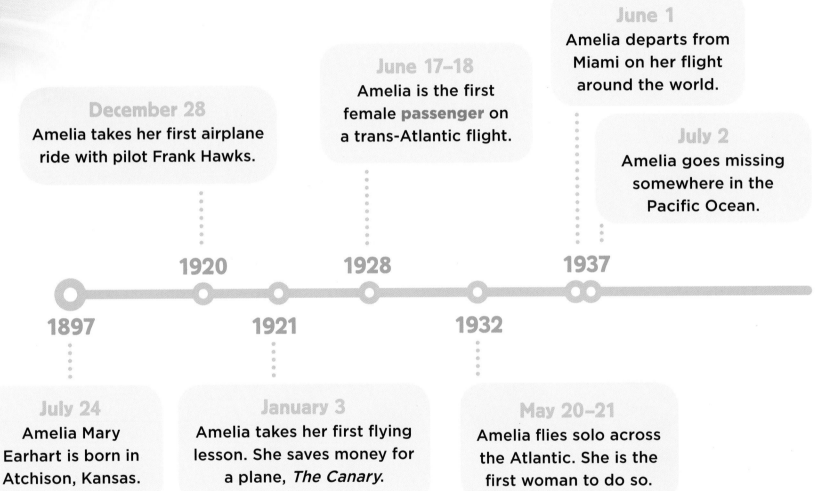

December 28
Amelia takes her first airplane ride with pilot Frank Hawks.

June 17–18
Amelia is the first female **passenger** on a trans-Atlantic flight.

June 1
Amelia departs from Miami on her flight around the world.

July 2
Amelia goes missing somewhere in the Pacific Ocean.

1920

1928

1937

1897

1921

1932

July 24
Amelia Mary Earhart is born in Atchison, Kansas.

January 3
Amelia takes her first flying lesson. She saves money for a plane, *The Canary*.

May 20–21
Amelia flies solo across the Atlantic. She is the first woman to do so.

Glossary

challenge – something that is hard to do.

navigator – a person who is skilled at directing an aircraft on the right course.

passenger – a person riding in a vehicle.

Index

abdokids.com

Use this code to log on to abdokids.com and access crafts, games, videos, and more!

Abdo Kids Code:
HAK1217